Life in the Gardens
Fräbel at Phipps

Printed in the United States of America
on FSC certified recycled paper with soy based ink.

Life in the Gardens

Hans Godo Fräbel, the world's most famous flamework glass artist and an avid gardener, is continuously inspired by nature and the world around him. In this book, you will see the exhibition that he and his team of glass artists have created with Phipps Conservatory and Botanical Gardens.

As beautiful as it is unusual, the artist's installation at Phipps brings a new and reflective view of garden–glass artistry to one of the oldest Victorian glasshouses in the country. Designed to whisk guests away to a dazzling fantasy world, the exhibition is filled with whimsical and otherworldly figures, mysterious masks, playful sculptures, and breathtaking botanical interplay – with backdrops designed by Scott Scarfone of Oasis Design Group in collaboration with Phipps staff. "When I first saw a Fräbel Longfellow in a garden, I knew we had to bring this exhibit to Phipps," said Richard V. Piacentini, Phipps executive director. "The interaction between these ethereal figures and the natural settings was like nothing I have ever seen before."

All exhibitions, like the one at Phipps Conservatory in Pittsburgh, are unique to their surrounding environments. For *Life in the Gardens*, Fräbel utilized Phipps' unique vegetation to optimally display his amazing glass sculptures and large scale installations.

Fräbel was so impressed with the Conservatory that he decided to introduce some incredible new installations to his botanical garden exhibition, inspired by, and made especially for, the Conservatory's dynamic architecture and distinctive progression of display rooms. New at this exhibition is the "Longfellow Gravity" installation, which consists of three large cubes that seem to tumble down a hill into a pond, surrounded by fourteen Longfellows in different sizes who playfully watch all of this happen. It is about seeing fun and enjoyment, even when things around you are not as easy as they once may have been. Further, Fräbel created his "Tower" installation, an enlarged version of his classic 1970s sculpture, "Tower of Babel".

Since the opening of the Fräbel Studio in 1968, flowers and plants have formed an important part of the Studio's realistic art repertoire. Flowers, like the Lily, Dogwood, Cherokee Rose and various Orchids, were recreated in realistic fashion using borosilicate glass. Wielding his creative expression, Fräbel has designed glass botanicals, interpreting the essence of plant life while displaying the magic and irresistible beauty of glass. After his initial

Longfellow, 2008
Photo by Paul g. Wiegman

visit to Phipps Conservatory and Botanical Gardens, Fräbel stated, "Phipps Conservatory is one of the oldest and largest conservatories in the US, and I am proud and honored to showcase my work in this beautiful setting. When you walk around this garden, you can just feel the history."

Life in the Gardens is the largest flamework glass art exhibition ever held in a botanical garden anywhere in the world and is organized by Phipps Conservatory and Botanical Gardens in cooperation with Hans Godo Fräbel.

History of the Phipps Conservatory and Botanical Gardens

Phipps Conservatory and Botanical Gardens

Phipps Conservatory and Botanical Gardens, a great steel and glass Victorian greenhouse, has been inviting visitors to explore the beauty and mysteries of plants since 1893. Set amidst one of Pittsburgh's largest greenspaces, Schenley Park, Phipps Conservatory stands as a cultural and architectural centerpiece in the city's Oakland neighborhood.

In recent decades, Phipps has evolved into one of the region's most vibrant, thriving cultural attractions, bringing fresh perspectives and artists into our historic glasshouse environment. Phipps has also become a strong advocate for advanced green-building practices, sustainable gardening and a new environmental awareness. An eco-champion among North America's 500 public gardens and ranked among the nation's top conservatory experiences, Phipps exhibits and programs have informed more than 3.5 million visitors since 1993 – including attendees from every state and 56 foreign countries – about the importance of plants and eco-harmony while leading all to the pleasures of the garden.

Phipps Conservatory was a gift to Pittsburgh by industrialist Henry Phipps, son of a Scottish immigrant cobbler. A friend and partner of Andrew Carnegie, Phipps made his fortune in steel and real estate, giving millions away in the tradition of philanthropy of the day. Today's Conservatory, the result of Phipps' endeavor to "erect something that will prove a source of instruction as well as pleasure to the people," is his best known legacy.

When the Conservatory opened on December 7, 1893, it was the largest and finest conservatory in the United States. A year later, when Phipps acquired a collection of rare plants from the World's Colombian Exposition in Chicago, it became distinguished as a repository of horticultural excellence, a reputation that continues today.

In 1993 Phipps was transferred from city to private nonprofit management in a move to sustain and advance its programs and in 1995 Phipps was named a contractual asset for funding from the newly formed Allegheny Regional Asset District. In 1998, the name of the organization was changed to Phipps Conservatory and Botanical Gardens to better reflect the broadening focus of its campus, exhibits and programs.

In recent years, Phipps has addressed public demand for a leader, advocate and information nexus for energy-efficiency in the built and natural environments by initiating a three-phase expansion of the Phipps campus. Expansion began in 2005 with the construction of a Silver LEED (Leadership in Energy and Environmental Design) certified Welcome Center – the first LEED certified building in a public garden. In December 2006, the Phipps expansion reached another milestone with the opening of the 12,000-square-foot Tropical Forest Conservatory – the most energy-efficient conservatory in the world and the nation's largest, changing-theme tropical forest display space. With new features including cascading indoor waterfalls, a canopy overlook, and interactive "research stations," the Tropical Forest brings a completely unique addition to the Phipps experience while incorporating a revolutionary heating and cooling approach that completely eliminates the greenhouse effect. The Phipps team accomplished this with a sweeping palette of energy-saving technologies and strategies that includes computer-controlled shading and ventilation, 1,800 feet of earth tubes, root-zone heating, thermal massing, and a solid oxide fuel cell. The Tropical Forest sets a new worldwide standard for energy-efficient conservatory construction and operation.

Phipps' ambitious plans now enter the third phase with the design and construction of the Center for Sustainable Landscapes (CSL) which will be a Living Building and one of the world's greenest buildings. A Living Building exceeds LEED Platinum, produces all of its own energy from renewable resources on site and treats all of its own water. The CSL will house leading-edge environmental education and research programs in a facility that is itself a working demonstration model of a variety of alternative, renewable energy strategies and devices – a public teaching tool, innovated with technically feasible, commercially viable technologies which can be replicated by others. In this way, Phipps is establishing a robust, transparent, and enlightening guest experience, spurring increased awareness and sounding a call to action for all who step through its doors. These improvements will distinguish Phipps as one of the most remarkable and finest conservatories in the world. Simultaneously, the enhancement of Phipps will further advance Pittsburgh and Pennsylvania's leadership role in green buildings, maintain a superior, family-centered quality of life for Western Pennsylvanians and stimulate our area's global competitiveness.

Aerial view of Phipps Conservatory and Botanical Gardens
Courtesy of Hawkeye Aerial Photo

Phipps embraces its new role of guiding the region it serves into a sustainable future through its very purpose and mission: *to inspire and educate visitors with the beauty and importance of plants, to advance sustainability and worldwide biodiversity through action and research, and to celebrate its historic glasshouse.*

All of this exciting development takes place within the context of continuing an over 100-year tradition of presenting outstanding horticultural displays and exhibits for the public. It is with this in mind that Phipps is pleased and proud to present *Life in the Gardens. Fräbel at Phipps.*

Richard V. Piacentini
EXECUTIVE DIRECTOR

Joseph F. Lagana
CHAIR, BOARD OF TRUSTEES

Hans Godo Fräbel and the Fräbel Studio

Hans Godo Fräbel was born in Jena, East Germany in 1941. He was the third child in a family with five children. The tumultuous political climate in existence after WWII necessitated a family migration to a small city called Wertheim in West Germany, where Fräbel's father opened a scientific glass factory with a business partner. After moving a few times, the family ended up in Mainz am Rhein, a much larger city in West Germany, where Fräbel's father obtained a position as a controller at the Jena Glaswerke. Fräbel did not enjoy school, and when 15 his father enrolled him into a "Lehrausbildung Program" (a traineeship) as a scientific glassblower at this prestigious company. Within 3 years, Fräbel received his "Gehilfenbrief," an apprenticeship diploma, showing that he had mastered the trade of scientific glass blowing.

In his spare time, he had the opportunity to focus on his real passion, art, and attended different art classes, to learn how to paint and draw.

In 1965 he came to the United States and settled in Atlanta. There he obtained a position at the Georgia Institute of Technology in its scientific glass blowing laboratory. There he also continued his art studies at Emory University and Georgia State University.

While working at Georgia Tech, Fräbel's creative talents were often sought after by professors and acquaintances alike to create crystal glass sculptures as gifts for friends, partners and business associates. With so many people enjoying the beauty of his glass sculptures, Fräbel felt strengthened to continue his quest to become an artist.

In the 1960's, glass was not accepted as an art medium yet and therefore, established art galleries decided not to represent glass artists. Because of this, Fräbel established his own glass studio in Atlanta, Georgia in 1968. Over the next 40 years, he would follow in accordance with the European tradition of apprentice and mentoring studio master: as the master artist he would pass his skills on to a handpicked group of apprentices, who after many years of training would become master artists in their own right.

Because glass was not considered an art medium in the 1960's, very few artists were utilizing the beauty and diversity that the techniques furnace glass and flame-worked glass offered to create unique art pieces.

Hans Godo Fräbel, 2008

Until that time, glass designers had always been giving their designs to factory glass workers, who would then try to create their design in glass. Harvey Littleton and Hans Godo Fräbel were among the first artists who chose glass as their art medium and decided to create glass art with their own hands.

Although Fräbel's art received much attention in the United States, his international breakthrough as a glass artist did not occur until 1979 when his pop art sculpture "Hammer and Nails" was utilized as the feature piece of the "New Glass Art Exhibition." For the next several years, the

ABSOLUT
Country of Sweden
VODKA

exhibition toured the world visiting museums in numerous major cities. This international exhibition was a major factor in the recognition of Hans Godo Fräbel as a founding father of modern torch-work in the world of art.

Over the years Fräbel's reputation as a master in glass art has spread worldwide beyond the glass community. Fräbel art pieces can be found in public and private collections in over 80 countries worldwide. Some of the more illustrious collectors of Fräbel glass art are Queen Elizabeth II, Emperor Akihito and Empress Michiko of Japan, current and former heads of governments such as Jimmy Carter, Ronald Reagan, Margaret Thatcher, Anwar Sadat as well as museums in London, Paris, Tokyo, Dresden, Valencia, Corning, San Francisco, New York and Washington D.C.

Some of the most famous Fräbels of all time are the "Hammer and Nails" sculpture from the "New Glass Art Exhibition" which is still traveling to museums around the world; and the playful, cavorting clowns which received worldwide recognition with the Absolut Vodka advertising campaign in the late 80's and early 90's. Hans Godo Fräbel was the first glass artist honored with the title of Absolut Artist. Other famous artists that were chosen as Absolut Artist are Andy Warhol and Keith Haring.

Until the mid 90's, the Fräbel Studio created art pieces almost exclusively in clear borosilicate, a strong, brilliant crystal that is resistant to scratches and which if broken can usually be restored without a trace of damage. In the mid 1990's the artists of the Fräbel Studio began exploring the use of color. Since that time, color has formed an increasingly important part of the Fräbel repertoire. Other techniques the Studio employs are sandblasting and painting. Sandblasting gives the sculpture a frosted, highlighted appearance, which is an interesting optical illusion. This optical illusion is produced by the human eye, which cannot handle the diffractions of the fine indentations in the glass. The indentations or facets on the surface of the glass reflect all colors of light from its surface and confuse the human eye, giving an impression of a whitish tint.

Sculptures created by Hans Godo Fräbel are signed with "GF," which stands for Godo Fräbel. These sculptures are one-of-a-kind exclusives or limited editions. Although an original study model has been created, it will never leave the Fräbel Studio. The mounting peg bears the year of its creation.

The Cavorting Clowns, 1987

The famed Cavorting Clowns sculpture that was utilized by the Absolut Vodka Company in their advertisements from 1987 until the early 1990's

Longfellow Gravity

Longfellow Gravity, 2009

This installation titled "Longfellow Gravity" is one of Hans Godo Fräbel's most recent creations and is making its debut at Phipps Conservatory.
It consists of 3 large cubes that seem to tumble down a hill into a pond, surrounded by 14 Longfellows in different sizes who continue to play while all of this is happening. Some of these "Longfellows" are about 4 feet tall.

Life in the Gardens. Fräbel at Phipps.

Clown Fountain

Cavorting Clown Fountain, 2006

Hans Godo Fräbel, renowned for his playful figures in glass, created this large fountain in 2006. Based on his illustrious Cavorting Clown theme, the fountain stands over 10' tall and 7' in diameter. The Cavorting Clown series brought international recognition to Fräbel when he was chosen as an Absolut Vodka Artist in 1987, the very first glass artist to be bestowed with this title. Other famous Absolut Vodka Artists are Andy Warhol and Keith Haring.

Hans Godo Fräbel in front of his "Cavorting Clown Fountain"
Phipps Conservatory and Botanical Gardens, 2009

Life in the Gardens. Fräbel at Phipps.

Masks

Masks, 1999

Hans Godo Fräbel has always been mesmerized with the theatre and he created this series of masks as a tribute to the performing arts. In his home, he has a large collection of masks from all over the world. The color in the glass is created by melting metal oxides in the glass. For instance, cobalt oxide gives glass a blue look and iron oxide gives a yellow look.

These unique masks are all hand created by Hans Godo Fräbel and after the masks are completed, sometimes without any color glass at all, the masks are laid in with actual gold and silver leaf, using a precious metal-to-glass bonding agent.

Masquerade, 2000
Photo by Paul g. Wiegman

Left:
Tragedy and Comedy, 2009

Right:
Poseidon's Mask, 2000

Longfellow Fountain

Longfellow Fountain, 2006

In 2002, Fräbel created a series of small and large "Longfellows". These elongated figures play with proportions by using exaggerated extremities and stretched torsos, giving these figures an almost alien look. The "Longfellows" in the "Longfellow Fountain" are the largest Fräbel has ever created, up to 44" tall. When light hits these sculptures, they light up at the ends and the thinner parts of the sculpture, creating a visual magic.

Tower

Tower, 2009

In the late 1970's, Hans Godo Fräbel created a small series of abstract sculptures of spheres connected to rods to create unique clear sculptures that create a beautiful play with light. This sculpture titled "Tower" is a large version of Fräbel's 1979 "Tower of Babel".

Balancing

Balancing, 2008

A lighthearted and playful portrayal of Hans Godo Fräbel's famous clowns. The message here is to enjoy life as if it is one big carnival. This installation consists of 13 clowns on large brightly colored spheres that freely float on the water. The clowns and spheres reflect delightfully in the water as the fountains gently move them.

Life in the Gardens. Fräbel at Phipps.

Photos by Donald M. Robinson

Life in the Gardens. Frabel at Phipps.

Goblets

Fantasy Flower Goblets, 2006

Fräbel Fantasy Flower Goblets are bright, colorful goblets, created to look lively like flowers. This entire series is based on real flowers that are around us on a daily basis.

Life in the Gardens. Fräbel at Phipps.

Large Cube with Imploded Spheres

Large Cube with
Imploded Glass Spheres, 2006

In the late 1970's, Hans Godo Fräbel created a small series of cube shaped abstracts, which were all between 15" and 30" in size. Based on these sculptures, Fräbel decided to try and create a cube as large as physically possible. Approximately 60 imploded spheres in the center of the cube generate a magnificent play with the sunlight.

Aces and Deuces, Jokers Wild

Aces and Deuces, Jokers Wild, 2008

This good-natured sculpture is a metaphor for life. Ups and downs; highs and lows. "Aces and Deuces, Jokers Wild". This installation by Hans Godo Fräbel represents the risks and challenges that we face and the gambles we have to make in our lives. It consists of 8 jokers balancing on large glass playing cards and should be seen both during the day time as well as night, when the spot lights give it a whole new dimension.

Life in the Gardens. Fräbel at Phipps.

Longfellows

Longfellows, 2006

The very first Longfellow Hans Godo Fräbel created was about 12" tall and was created immediately out of glass. No sketches were made to design the first Longfellow. These elongated figures play with proportions by using exaggerated extremities and stretched torsos, giving these figures an almost alien look.

Life in the Gardens. Fräbel at Phipps.

Vineys & Sprites

Blue Trumpet Flower with Opaque Sprite, 1999

Fräbel's Viney sculptures blend the human form with plant life and represent the close-knit connection between humans and nature. Fräbel first started creating these unique figures in 1997.

Sprites are sculptures that mix nature and fantasy by depicting sprites (the male version of fairies) dancing on branches and flowers.

Red & Amber
Trunk Woman Viney, 1999

Green Branch
with 5 opaque Sprites, 1998

Red & White Trunk
Woman Viney, 2009

Frogs and Lizards

Oriental Fire Bellied Toad, 2008

These frogs are all endangered or extinct tropical frogs, most of them from South or Central America. The frog series were originally inspired during an exhibition of the works of Hans Godo Fräbel at the Atlanta Botanical Garden, which has its own endangered frog program to try to rescue these endangered frogs from extinction.

The fantasy lizards shown in this chapter will never be found in real life. Each and every one of these creations are dervied from the imagination of Hans Godo Fräbel's mind.

Blue Lizards, 2006

Spurell's Leaf Frog, 2006

Brown Lizards, 2006

Wavy Bowls

Wavy Bowl, 2006

Fräbel's wavy bowls are strings of borosilicate glass that all connect to create a bowl-like structure. All the connections and the thin pieces of glass create an incredible play with the sunlight.

Life in the Gardens [illegible]pps.

Life in the Gardens. Fräbel at Phipps.

Winter

Winter, 2009

This Fräbel Winter display features over 200 wintery looking glass sculptures, such as various designs of Snowflakes and a number of shaped imploded blown sculptures. For over 15 years, Fräbel has designed a limited edition Snowflake for the Holiday Season and all of these unique designs are on display here. Each Snowflake is limited to an edition of 100 and they are normally sold out by early November.

Life in the Gardens. Fräbel at Phipps.

Water Lilies, Lotuses and Orchids

Ghost Orchid, 2006

Hans Godo Fräbel's breathtaking Orchids, Water Lilies and Lotuses. All of these flowers are exact replicas of actual flowers and most of the Orchids are rare or extinct. They are brought to life in glass by the incredible art of Hans Godo Fräbel.

Nelumbo Sacred Lotus, 2008

Left:
Nymphaea Mrs. Charles Winch, 2008

Right:
Encyclia Tampensis, 2008

Nymphaea Lindsay Wood, 2008

Life in the Gardens. Fräbel at Phipps.

Nelumbo Lutea, 2008

Fräbel Studio
689-695 Antone St. NW
Atlanta, Georgia 30318

Tel 404.351.9794
Fax 404.351.1491

www.frabel.com

Phipps Conservatory and Botanical Gardens
One Schenley Park
Pittsburgh, PA 15213

Tel 412.622.6914
Fax 412.665.2368

phipps.conservatory.org